A Writers' Compendium

ℭℬ   ℬↄ

More Nonfiction by Peter Bollen

The Great Labor Quotations: Sourcebook and Reader

"Rest assured, this book will occupy a prized place in my library."
—Cesar Chavez

"You have given voice to proud generations."
—Victor Reuther

"I'm greatly impressed."
—George Seldes

"You solved my speech writing problem."
—Ed Asner

"A worthy project—should be read and pondered by working people everywhere."
—Studs Terkel

Frank Talk: The Wit and Wisdom of Barney Frank

Stephen Colbert's List of Bests

"I'm deeply flattered—and for doing it so well."
—Barney Frank

Nuclear Voices: A Book of Quotations and Perspectives

"It is a very impressive accomplishment."
—John Kerry

"A fine and valuable contribution to the literature of survival in this age."
—Mario Cuomo

"Although the volume's bias is pronounced, those who share it will be edified by these observations."
—Booklist

"I think it's a wonderful project."
—Stephen King

A Writers' Compendium

Quotations on the Trade

Edited and Compiled by Peter Bollen

Art by Ramona du Houx

Polar Bear & Company
An imprint of the
Solon Center for Research and Publishing
Solon, Maine

To the late George Seldes,
mentor, friend and hero

Polar Bear & Company™
Solon Center for Research and Publishing
PO Box 311, Solon, ME 04979, U.S.A.
207.643.2795, polarbearandco.org, soloncenter.org

ISBN: 978-1-882190-78-2
Cover, art and design by Ramona du Houx.
First print edition, first printing December 2017
Library of Congress Control Number: 2017960325
Manufactured on durable, acid-free paper in more than one country.

Contents

Editor's Note

As a longtime literary book collector, I have concentrated on writers' memoirs and biographies, as well as interviews and conversations with a wide range of writers working in various fields. This obsession became my education for my own writing and my career in publishing. Gleaning all this literary wisdom fueled my desire to compile a useful and entertaining collection of literary nuggets for readers and anyone who aspires to write. Putting this volume together and reading the words of these lively minds on the craft of writing and the creative process was particularly enjoyable and personally edifying.

The chapters in this book include quotations on creativity, censorship, critiques from fellow writers, and the importance of journalism. I hope they convey something about the writing life and the value of the printed word.

I intend for this collection to serve as a helpful guide for aspiring and fledgling writers. I have included a chapter on the dreaded writer's block—that familiar malady suffered, at times, by even the most experienced wordsmiths. When I interview and talk with writers personally, I always ask them about The Block.

I hope this compendium is entertaining as well as useful for readers and writers alike.

Acknowledgments

I have been influenced by many writers and other journalists during my years as a Labor journalist and freelance writer. In my current position as editor at Highland/Hillside Books, I have compiled several collections of quotations focused on specific themes.

My fascination with the writing process and sharing the vicissitudes of fellow wordsmiths inspired me to compile this writers' compendium. Writers in all fields experience the ups and downs of the craft: the stress of working with publishing deadlines, the joy of completing assignments, the agony of dealing with critics, and the esprit de corps of commiserating with literary colleagues. What binds us together is our love for the craft of writing. This collection aims to celebrate all those who share a fascination with the written word.

I am grateful to the staffs of several organizations for which I have had the privilege of writing and editing, including the Northeast News Service of the Postal Press Association. I want to thank Janet Groth for permission to quote from her memoir, *The Receptionist* (Algonquin Books). I also wish to extend my gratitude to Jodi Picoult, Carolyn Chute, Sara Gruen, and syndicated columnist Ellen Goodman for permission to quote. Special thanks to Perri Black.

Finally, I would be woefully remiss if I failed to acknowledge and thank my dear friends and family for putting up with my occasional self-imposed isolation and for understanding and tolerating the motivations and daily habits of a dedicated "ink-stained wretch."

There's no rule on how it is to write. Sometimes it comes easily and perfectly. Sometimes it is like drilling rock and then blasting it out with charges.

— Ernest Hemingway

Chapter One

The Process

There's no rule on how it is to write. Sometimes it comes easily and perfectly. Sometimes it is like drilling rock and then blasting it out with charges.

— Ernest Hemingway

It's always a challenge how to begin, how to get into it and interest a reader. I spend a lot of time thinking about the first paragraph, and sometimes I spend a couple of days on the first sentence.

— Alan Lightman

Ours is the most solitary of occupations; the only comparison I can think of is keeper of a lighthouse . . . But the analogy mustn't go too far; we do not cast the beam of light that will save the individual, or the world from coming to grief on its rocks.

—Nadine Gordimer

Writing, in my experience, consists of long periods of hanging out, punctuated by the fugue of remorse at the loss of one's powers and wonder at occasional output in spite of that loss.

— David Mamet

If you haven't always been doing it, you haven't always wanted it.

— George V. Higgins

An artist is his own fault.

— John O'Hara

No one asks you to write, and no one will care if you stop. And if you succeed, no one will notice. It's a rough, heartless business.

— George V. Higgins, speaking to writing students

Read everything.

— E. L. Doctorow, advice to aspiring writers

When still a child, make sure you read a lot of books. Spend more time doing this than anything else.

— Zadie Smith

Writing a column is easy. All I do is open a vein, and it comes out one drop at a time.

— Red Smith

Bringing order out of disorder is a female function.

— P. D. James

A diary, if intended for publication (and how many written by a novelist are not?), is the most egotistical form of writing.

— P. D. James

For things that are not known—at least not anymore—and that there is now no way of finding out about, one has to fall back on imagination. This is not the same thing as the truth, but neither is it necessarily a falsehood.

— William Maxwell, explaining his fiction

I came, as a result of being an editor, to look for whatever was unnecessary in my own writing. After 40 years, what I came to care about most was not style, but the breath of life.

— William Maxwell

I write entirely to find out what I'm thinking, what I'm looking at, what I see and what it means.

— Joan Didion

I don't think that one is impressed with one's own work. I can't imagine such a thing. It's a question of getting it right; it's not a question of admiring it.

— Mavis Gallant

I find that anger—a sense of outrage—can be liberating for the creative process—if it is disciplined. Anger improves lucidity, persistence, audacity and apathy.

— Jack Newfield

I'm always looking for the blanks in the historical canvas—the people and things nobody really knows about.

— Louis Bayard

What distinguishes a classic from an ordinary book is, of course, authority, and to write with . . . authority you have to have a great deal to say and no hesitation about how it is to be said or about saying it.

— William Maxwell

The professional writer who spends his time becoming other people and places, real or imaginary, finds he has written his life away and become almost nothing.

— V. S. Pritchett

If you can imagine the sheer bloody pleasure of having an idea and taking it! It's one of the great pleasures in my life. My God, an idea!

— Doris Lessing

1. The Process

There is, I am sure, a direct connection between passionate love and the firing of the creative power of the mind.

— V. S. Pritchett

Where there is nothing but rejections, then the writer can only conclude that he is a misunderstood genius or should be in another line of work.

— William Maxwell

You can only write regularly if you're willing to write badly. You can't write regularly and well. One should accept bad writing as a way of priming the pump, a warm-up exercise that allows you to write well.

— Jennifer Egan

Take care that you never spell a word wrong. Always before you write a word, consider how it is spelt, and if you do not remember it, turn to a dictionary. It produces great praise to a lady to spell well.

— Thomas Jefferson

After twenty commercial publishing houses have turned down a book, I try a small press. When you love a book, you can't give up.

— Ellen Levine, agent

You have to keep writing, keep submitting, and keep praying to the God of whimsey that some editor will respond favorably.

— Peter Benchley

In the end it's up to you. I'd say that in today's tough publishing climate, you have to want to be a writer very, very much in order to succeed.

— Joseph Hansen

Humor is the secret weapon of the nonfiction writer. It is secret because so few writers realize that it is often their best tool—for making an important point.

— William Zinsser

I believe what makes books sell, more than anything else, is word of mouth.

— Nora Ephron

Literature is, perhaps, the most powerful of the arts.

— James T. Farrell

Writing a novel is like building a wall brick by brick; only amateurs believe in inspiration.

— Frank Yerby

The most essential gift for a good writer is a built-in, shockproof shit detector.

— Ernest Hemingway

I leave out the parts that people skip.

— Elmore Leonard

The problem for a self-respecting writer is that the act of writing almost in its nature promises something new. Repetition is not really writing but propaganda—not illumination for the mind but a mental beating.

— Jonathan Schell

School is where most contemporary writers chiefly developed their love of reading, that necessary prerequisite for the then burgeoning desire to write.

— George V. Higgins

We do it for the hell of it, and those who raise a lot of hell, and then get very lucky, well, we make a living, too. There are worse ways to travel through this vale of tears than by doing the things you love, and making a living at it.

— George V. Higgins

Morning after morning for 50 years, I faced the next page defenseless and unprepared. Writing for me was a feat of self-preservation. If I did not do it, I would die. So I did it.

— Philip Roth

I love to play with the idea of the unreliable narrator. Keep them alert—that's my motto about readers.

— Peter Taylor, advice to his students

A writer with an audience has more power than most congressmen.

— Gore Vidal

Thank goodness I can still write. When you get too old to do anything else, you'll still have that.

— Peter Taylor

Compression is everything.

— Peter Taylor's dictum

If you don't have time to read, you don't have the time or the tools to write.

— Stephen King

During the visit the owner said to me, "Now you're not going to write anything about this house, are you?" And I said, "Oh no, sir." Then about ten years later, I started describing it in a story—a writer will use anything.

— Peter Taylor

Literature is really the attempt to give shape to something that has no shape.

— Gore Vidal

And art itself may be defined as a single-minded attempt to render the highest kind of justice to the visible universe, by bringing to light the truth, manifold and one, underlying its every aspect.

— Joseph Conrad

Where is this coming from? I sometimes wonder. Oh, it is interesting, the creative process. Where was this story before I wrote it down? I don't know.

— Gore Vidal

The usual short story cannot have a complex plot, but it often has a simple one resembling a chain with two or three links.

— Irving Howe

Omit needless words.

— William Strunk Jr. and E. B. White
The Elements of Style

We are writers, and we never ask one another where we get our ideas; we know we don't know.

— Stephen King

I share the mystery with fellow writers of where our stories come from.
— Martin Amis, attributed

The power of fiction lies in its capacity to gaze upon this odd circumstance of our existence, to allow us to play with the conundrum that we are making ourselves up as we go along.

— Mohsin Hamid

A writer who understands the artificial nature of reality is more or less obliged to enter the process of making it.

— Salman Rushdie

Be regular and orderly in your life, like a bourgeois, so that you may be violent and original in your work.

— Gustave Flaubert

A book ought to be an ax to break up the frozen sea within us.

— Franz Kafka

Nothing is indescribable.

— Harold Ross, original editor of *The New Yorker*

Never use a verb other than "said" to carry dialogue . . . I once noticed Mary McCarthy ending a line of dialogue with "she asservated," and had to stop reading and go to the dictionary.

— Elmore Leonard

Many of us felt that Ken was ruthless. He kept hammering it into our skulls that writing was Work, with no easy way out. To function it had to be hewn, carved, sweated and driven into shape.

— Noel Young, student of Kenneth Millar whose pseudonym was Ross MacDonald,

I loved that magazine so much I concentrated all my wishing into an effort to make myself small and inky and intense enough to be received into its pages.

— John Updike, before writing for
The New Yorker

A student of cultural history is the last person to believe he is self-made or the sole begetter of his most original idea.

— Jacques Barzun

It's always a push to get up the stairs, to sit down and go to work. You'd rather do almost anything, read the paper again, write some letters, play with your old dust jackets, any number of things you'd rather do than tackle that empty page, because what you do on the page is you, your ticket to all the good luck you've enjoyed.

— John Updike

I aim in my mind not toward New York but toward a vague spot a little to the east of Kansas.

— John Updike

Narrative imagination—and therefore fiction—is a basic evolutional tool of survival. We process the world by telling stories and produce human knowledge through our engagement with imagined selves.

— Alexsandar Hemon

A novel is primarily a presentation of human beings in action. The difference between the so-called art novel and the popular variety is perhaps that in the first the human beings are more important than the action and in the second it is the other way about.

— Anthony Burgess

I'm a storyteller. I never know what's going to be in the next line, the next paragraph, or the next page.

— Jeffrey Archer

A work that aspires, however humbly, to the condition of art should carry its justification in every line. And art itself may be defined as a single-minded attempt to render the highest kind of justice to the visible universe, by bringing to light the truth, manifold and one, underlying its every aspect.

— Joseph Conrad

One afternoon I wrote some words while sitting in an old barn looking out on the mountain; and these words were "I'm an invisible man." I didn't know quite what they meant, and I didn't know where the idea came from . . . then after that, it was a process of trying to make a meaningful story out of what seemed to be a rather wild notion.

— Ralph Ellison

I have been told, both in approval and in accusation, that I seem to love all my characters. What I do in writing of any character is to try to enter into the mind, heart, and skin of a human being who is not myself . . . It is the act of a writer's imagination that I set most high.

— Eudora Welty

Most smart people tend to feel queasy when the conversation turns to things like "certain death" and "total failure" and the idea of a "doomed generation." But not me. I am comfortable with these themes.

— Hunter S. Thompson

Writing begins in obsession. It might be an obsession with a beloved (think Dante) or craft (think Bishop), or even with obsession itself (think Nabokov). There seems to be an elective affinity between the writer and the obsessive. Both see the world as more beautiful and terrifying, more dramatic and meaningful, than the rest of us do.

— Anthony Domestico

Being a writer is like having homework every night for the rest of your life.

— Lawrence Kasdan

I became a foreigner. For myself that is what a writer is—a man living on the other side of a frontier.

— V. S. Pritchett, on leaving his native England as a young man to explore his literary ambition

1. The Process

The critical essay is never a lecture but a conversation.
— V. S. Pritchett, attributed

I don't think that a writer like myself, an imaginative writer, should put whatever talent he or she has at the service of a revolution, no matter how much you believe in it yourself . . . but I think that if you distort whatever little talent you've been given, that's wrong, because talent is the one thing you have and it should be used faithfully in dealing with the world around you.
— Nadine Gordimer

I see all fiction as truth-telling, and all fiction as social history: a history of the psyche in its time.
— Nadine Gordimer

Fiction is a clarifying agent. It makes truth plausible. Among all the means of communication now available, imaginative literature comes closer than any other to being able to give an impression of the truth.
— John Hersey

It is our inward journey that leads us through time—forward or back, seldom in a straight line, most often spiraling.
— Eudora Welty

A writer is, on the whole, most alive when alone.
— Martin Amis, attributed

I guess I think I'm writing for people who are smarter than I am because then I'll be doing something that's worth their time.

— Susan Sontag

A lot of critics think I'm stupid because my sentences are so simple and my method is so direct: they think these are defects. No. The point is to write as much as you know as quickly as possible.

— Kurt Vonnegut

When you start any book, you don't know what, ultimately, your issues are. You try to write to find them. You're fiddling with the stuff, hoping to make sense, whatever kind of sense you can make.

— Robert Penn Warren

I just don't outline. I follow the scent . . . You know the direction you're going in, but you don't know how you'll get there.

— Flannery O'Connor

I finish hanging the laundry and go up to the typewriter and sit there, holding my head trying to quiet my head. You see, I can't just switch from life mode to writer mode. Usually it takes three days to get into the writer mode. Three days of quiet non-life mode, lots of coffee and no interruptions.

— Carolyn Chute

I write to reveal my way of being in the world, my sensibility.

— Zadie Smith, attributed

I'm a big Scrabble player, and I used to write puzzles . . . Sometimes I think of writing as being like that: cryptic, filled with clues, inscrutable, elegant.

— Meg Wolitzer

Sometimes a manuscript is like bread dough. You have to abuse it.

— Carolyn Chute

If writing were illegal, I'd be in prison. I can't not write. It's a compulsion.

— David Baldacci

When I'm writing I have total control . . . There's no time when I'm more content, more at ease, than when it's just me alone in a room for eight hours.

— James Frey

I do feel like I'm on Pluto sometimes, just watching how people treat each other. And when I write, I just let my characters go.

— Carolyn Chute

We have a natural right to
make use of our pens as of
our tongue, at our peril, risk
and hazard.

—Voltaire,
Philosophical Dictionary, 1764

Every book teaches you the lessons necessary to write that book.

— Eudora Welty, attributed

There are no secrets and there are no shortcuts. As an aspiring writer, what you need to know is that learning to write is self-taught, and learning to write well takes years.

— Sue Grafton

There's a moment in every book when the story and characters are finally there; they come to life, they're in control. They do things they're not supposed to do and become people they weren't meant to be. When I reach that place, it's magic. It's a kind of rapture.

— Sara Gruen

Every time I start a book I have to put my horseshoe down and arrange my stones within it until it feels right. And then I don't touch them again until I finish the book. If I feel the need to rearrange the rocks while I'm writing, that's a symptom of a pretty bad block.

— Sara Gruen

I'm a little bit superstitious. As I said, everything I do with my writing is ritualized. After I check my e-mail, I get another cup of tea. I check my e-mail again. And then I shut down the Internet and open my file.

— Sara Gruen

For me, writing is inseparable from thinking. I could say the entire undertaking is a vast cerebral construct against my demons. It's the thing that I love. It's my identity.

— Kathryn Harrison

When I'm writing I'm unaware of myself. I'm in my characters, in the story. I know the writing is going well when I look at my watch and see that it's ten p.m., and the last time I looked it was noon.

— Gish Gen

Writing is a ridiculous thing to do for money. If you do it, do it for the reason writers have always done it, which is not money but for another, deeper satisfaction.

— Gish Gen

There are musicians who talk about a solo they've done and they have no idea where that came from. There are athletes who set world records and say, "I performed so far outside my abilities, I don't know what that was." It happens to writers, too. That's the thing we're all looking for. That's the drug.

— Sebastian Junger

Ever tried. Ever failed. No matter. Try again. Fail better.

— Samuel Beckett, attributed

There's no simple explanation for why I write. It changes over time. There's no hole inside me to fill or anything like that, but once I started doing it, I couldn't imagine wanting to do anything else for a living.

— Michael Lewis

Tell the truth through whichever veil comes to hand—but tell it. Resign yourself to the lifelong sadness that comes from never being satisfied.

— Zadie Smith

I write to explain myself. It's a way of processing my disasters, sorting out the messiness of life to lend symmetry and meaning to it.

— Armistead Maupin

Why do I write? To do better for myself than I am capable of doing with language, out there, in real time. To repair inabilities, to restore confidences.

— Rick Moody

I didn't choose to write. It was something that just happened to me. I write to shed dead skin and to explore why people do the things that we do to each other and to ourselves.

— Terry McMillan

People sometimes ask if I know what my characters are up to at any given moment. No, of course not. But I know how to find them once again. I just tap into whatever aspect of my own personality helped me identify them in the first place.

— Armistead Maupin

Writing is the act of saying I, of imposing oneself upon other people, of saying listen to me, see it my way, change your mind.

— Joan Didion, attributed

I write to meet my ghosts.

— Terry Tempest Williams, attributed

The worst moment in a writer's life is the perpetual recurring moment, and that's rejection. If you keep writing what you want to write, you're going to get a lot of rejection.

— Walter Mosley

Rejection is always painful, but you learn to enjoy it . . . You love to get together with other writers and talk about the worst rejection you ever had.

— Walter Mosley

Thomas Edison is not one of my favorite guys, but he said, "Genius is one percent inspiration, ninety percent perspiration." He was right.

— Walter Mosley

I don't treat myself as this precious flower. The fact that writing is a job doesn't undercut the fact that it's also an art.

— Susan Orlean

Don't be ashamed to use the thesaurus. I could spend all day reading Roget's! There's nothing better when you're in a hurry and you need the right word right now.

— Susan Orlean

Staying focused, sitting at your desk, is your number one job as a writer. There's always something else to do. Don't do it! Remember, time applied equals work completed.

— Ann Patchett

Sometimes it's magical . . . at a certain point in every book, something happens that I never saw coming—at least, not consciously—and it's exactly the puzzle piece the story is missing, the element that ties the threads of the book together. Characters seem to pick their own paths.

— Jodi Picoult

I write because I swear to God I don't know how to do anything else.

— Ann Patchett

Order and simplification are the first steps toward the mastery of a subject.

— Thomas Mann

Even though I know the end of my books before writing a single word, I often find that the middle section—how I get from point A to point Z—is a delightful surprise.

— Jodi Picoult

There's no magic bullet that'll make you a success. If you write because you want to be rich, you're in the wrong business. Write because you can't not write, or don't write at all.

— Jodi Picoult

If you're curious, there's always a subject to write about.

— Jane Smiley

I write in different styles because I hear different voices in my head. It would be boring to have always the same voice, point of view.

— Gore Vidal

The writing of a novel is taking life as it already exists, not to report it but to make it an object, toward the end that the finished work might contain this life inside it and offer it to the reader. The essence will not be, of course, the same thing as the raw material . . . The novel is something that never was before and will not be again.

— Eudora Welty

The first sentence can't be written until the final sentence is written.

— Joyce Carol Oates

When your story is ready for rewrite, cut it to the bone. Get rid of every ounce of excess fat. This is going to hurt; revising a story down to the bare essentials is always a little like murdering children, but it must be done.

— Stephen King

Genius gives birth, talent delivers.

— Jack Kerouac

A person who publishes a book willfully appears before the populace with his pants down.

— Edna St. Vincent Millay, attributed

Humiliations are suffered by most writers most of the time—a writer's humiliations are chicken feed as compared with those endured by people who work for a living, and are grateful simply to make it home at night. Writers are already home.

— Roger Rosenblatt

I work hard, I work very hard. All the books at least 30 revisions.

— Ha Jin, attributed

When I'm looking for an idea, I'll do anything—clean the closet, mow the lawn, work in the garden.

— Kevin Henkes, attributed

Ideas are the cheapest part of the writing. They are free. The hard part is what you do with ideas you've gathered.

— Jane Yolen, attributed

I rewrite a great deal. I'm always fiddling, always changing something. I'll write a few words—then I'll change them. I add. I subtract. I work and fiddle and keep working and fiddling, and I only stop at deadline.

— Ellen Goodman

I hate to advocate drugs, alcohol, violence, or insanity to anyone, but they've always worked for me.

— Hunter S. Thompson, attributed

A writer's greatest pleasure is revealing to people things they knew, but did not know they knew.

— Andy Rooney

What I've always hoped to do with my writing is to say, in so many words, some of the ideas that lurk, wordlessly, in the minds of a great many people.

— Andy Rooney

Characters are not created by writers. They preexist, and they have to be found. If we do not find them, if we fail to represent them, the fault is ours.

— Elizabeth Bowen, attributed

One can't tell writers what to do. The imagination must find its own path.

— Saul Bellow

When your story is ready for rewrite, cut it to the bone. Get rid of every ounce of excess fat. This is going to hurt; revising a story down to the bare essentials is always a little like murdering children, but it must be done.

— Stephen King

I used to do my writing forty years ago on yellow second sheets from the five-and-dime, and I became attached to this coarse yellow paper, which caught the tip of the pen and absorbed too much ink.

— Saul Bellow

Try to be one of those people on whom nothing is lost.

— Henry James, advice to apprentice novelists, attributed

The constants that I look for are a love of light and a determination to trace some moral chain of being.

— John Cheever

Ideas come in two different ways—conscious ideas acquired through education and reading, and things that pop into your head willy-nilly.

— Keith Botsford

Never be afraid to raise your voice for honesty and truth and compassion against injustice and lying and greed. If people all over the world . . . would do this, it would change the earth.

— William Faulkner, attributed

Before I start to write, I always treat myself to a nice dry martini. Just one, to give me the courage to get started. After that, I am on my own.

— E. B. White

What I write when I force myself is generally just as good as what I write when I'm feeling inspired. It's mainly a matter of forcing yourself to write.

— Tom Wolfe

Avoid clichés like the plague.

— Samuel Goldwyn

Words can sometimes, in moments of grace, attain the quality of deeds.

— Elie Wiesel

I'm very particular about pens and paper. I use those Rhodia notebooks with the orange cover [and] graph paper.

— Claire Messud

I suppose I write because I want to reach people and by reaching them, influence the history of my time a little bit.

— Norman Mailer

What makes a novelist great is that he illumines each line of his work with the greatest intensity of experience.

— Norman Mailer

I had hundreds of books under my skin already. Not selected reading, all of it. Some of it could be called trashy. I had been through Nick Carter, Horatio Alger, Bertha M. Clay and the whole slew of dime novelists in addition to some really constructive reading. I do not regret the trash. It has harmed me in no way. It was a help, because acquiring the reading habit early is the important thing. Taste and natural development will take care of the rest later on.

—Zora Neale Hurston

I believe more in the scissors than I do in the pencil.
— Truman Capote

It is the actions of men and not their sentiments which make history— the best sentence I've ever written—but I would hate to face eternity with that for my flag, since I am still at this formal middle of my life a creator of sentiments larger than my work.
— Norman Mailer

Talent is cheaper than table salt. What separates the talented individual from the successful one is a lot of hard work.
— Stephen King

If there's a book you really want to read, but it hasn't been written yet, then you must write it.
— Toni Morrison

To be a writer is to throw away a great deal, not to be satisfied, to type again, and then again, and once more, and over and over . . .

— John Hersey

The most valuable of all talents is that of never using two words when one will do.

— Thomas Jefferson

If you want to be a writer, write . . . Save everything you write. If you feel blocked, write through it until you feel your creative juices flowing again. Write.

— Anne Rice

Reading, the love of reading, is what makes you dream of becoming a writer.

— Susan Sontag

I just write what I wanted to write. I write what amuses me. It's totally for myself.

— J. K. Rowling

[I write] to amuse mankind, to help the sick and the dull and the weary.
— Arthur Conan Doyle, attributed

Honest autobiography is therefore a contradiction in terms.
— H. L. Mencken

If you are going to write autobiography, don't expect that it will clear anything up. It makes it more clear to you, but it doesn't alleviate anything.

— Maya Angelou

Nothing the human race has ever invented is more cool than a book.
— Tom Robbins

A writer's primary function is, first, to help buoy up the human spirit in an existential world, in a genuine way, by exhibiting characters, including himself. Second, his work has to have some unity, some purpose.
— Henry Roth

Writing well is the best revenge.
— Ross Macdonald, attributed

Fiction is the lost art of transforming the personal and specific into the common and universal.

— Ken Millar

The most fruitful thing for a writer to do was quiet brooding.

— John Galsworthy, attributed

We are the sum of all the moments of our lives.

— Thomas Wolfe

That transition between writing and not writing is the hardest transition on earth.

— Lily King

Read what makes you happy. Or unhappy. Or curious. Or uncomfortable. It's your reading life.

— Hillary Kelly

There is nothing more substantial to place against the cruelty of the world than language.

— Colum McCann

Creativity is not like a freight train going down the tracks. It's something that has to be caressed and treated with a great deal of respect. If your mind is intellectually in the way, it will stop you.

— Bob Dylan

Rewriting is the essence of writing.

— William Zinsser

I have spent a good many years since—too many, I think—being ashamed about what I write. I think I was forty before I realized that almost every writer of fiction or poetry who has ever published a line has been accused by someone of wasting his or her God-given talent. If you write (or paint or dance or sculpt or sing, I suppose), someone will try to make you feel lousy about it, that's all.

— Stephen King

A writer will do anything to avoid the act of writing.

— William Zinsser

Humor is the secret weapon of the nonfiction writer.

— William Zinsser

You must learn by imitation.

— S. J. Perelman, attributed

I am one of the rare breed of writers who believes that the best part of writing is creating situations in which language can happen. I have to surround the act of writing with an aura of surprise and terror.

— Tom Robbins

Writing is the thing that pervades my whole day—I'm always wondering how I might describe something or improve my understanding, I'm constantly trying to remember an eavesdropped conversation or an idea for a story.

— Emma Healey

Clutter is the official language used by the American corporation—in its news release and its annual report—to hide its mistakes.

— William Zinsser

The essay is a weapon against the degenerate tendencies of the age. The novel, properly conceived, is a means of uplifting the spirit; its aim is to inspire, not merely to satisfy the low curiosity of man in man.

— H. L. Mencken

I write because in the act of creation there comes that mysterious abundant sense of being both parent and child; I am giving birth to an Other and simultaneously being reborn as child in the playground of creation.

— Francine du Plessix Gray

I write because I don't know what I think until I read what I say.

— Flannery O'Connor, attributed

I spend a great deal of time thinking about the power of language— the way it can evoke an emotion, a visual image, a complex idea, or a simple truth.

— Amy Tan

If the growing corp of popular science writers would focus on how scientists develop and defend those fascinating claims, they would make their greatest possible contribution to public understanding.

— Stephen Jay Gould

Language is the only homeland.

— Czeslaw Milosz

Political language—and with variations this is true of all political parties, from Conservatives to Anarchists—is designed to make lies sound truthful and murder respectable, and to give an appearance of solidity to pure wind.

— George Orwell

In order for a woman to write fiction she must have two things, certainly: a room of her own (with key and lock) and enough money to support herself.

— Virginia Woolf

But what argument can one make against a slur—even one that is not anonymous? If anything, an epithet is designed to short-circuit rationality, to inflame feelings, to draw a curtain, the color of boiling blood, across the life of the mind.

— Leslie Epstein

I think a man is doing his reporting well only when people start to hate him.

— V. S. Naipal

Words are sacred. They deserve respect. If you get the right ones, in the right order, you can nudge the world a little.

— Tom Stoppard

After years of reading manuscripts, I've developed megalogomania: fear of writing big words. I'm hoping it's contagious.

— Jessica Page Morrell

Plot is characters under stress.

— Henry James

The conscious mind is the editor, and the subconscious mind is the writer. And the joy of writing, when you're writing from your subconscious, is beautiful—it's thrilling.

— Steve Martin

The stupid believe that to be truthful is easy; only the artist knows how difficult it is.

— Willa Cather

Art should not reflect culture; art should subvert culture.

— Bob Dylan, attributed

In order for a writer to be productive, there must be a burning desire to communicate something to someone. Without the inspiration, it is all too easy not to write.

— Ria Biley

The writer is of service to humankind only insofar as the writer uses the word even against his or her own loyalties.

— Nadine Gordimer

Style is that façade a writer erects to conceal his voice.

— Lawrence Block

Get an agent, get an agent, get an agent.

— Robert B. Parker to
crime writer Jeremiah Healy

Beginners sometime ask me how a novel is written, the answer to which is: anyway at all.

— Thomas Berger

Why does one write? Because it isn't there! Unlike Everest and other celebrated eminences.

— Thomas Berger

1. The Process

It took me fifteen years to discover that I had no talent for writing, but I couldn't give it up because by that time I was too famous.

— Robert Benchley

About the only originality than any writer can hope to achieve honestly is to steal with good judgment.

— Josh Billings

Cats are dangerous companions for writers because cat watching is a near-perfect method of writing avoidance.

— Dan Greenberg

The act of writing is the act of discovering what you believe.

— David Hare

The novelist, afraid his ideas may be foolish, slyly puts them in the mouth of some other fool and reserves the right to disavow them.

— Diane Johnson

Your manuscript is both good and original; but the part that is good is not original, and the part that is original is not good.

— Samuel Johnson

Writing is not hard. Just get paper and pencil, sit down, and write it as it occurs to you. The writing is easy—it's the recurring that's hard.

— Stephen Leacock

Literature is mostly about having sex and not much about having children; life is the other way round.

— David Lodge

It is only in literature that coincidences seem unnatural.

— Robert Lynd

If you steal from one author, it's plagiarism; if you steal from many, it's research.

— Wilson Mizner

Any event, once it has occurred, can be made to appear inevitable by a competent historian.

— Lee Simonson

Income tax returns are the most imaginative fiction being written today.

— Herman Wouk

In schools where I used to patrol the toilets, I am today required reading.

— Bel Kaufman

I had learned, I suppose, the first lesson of agenting: the pitch.
— Joanna Rakoff, on submitting a story to an agent

The worst that being an artist could do to you would be that it would make you slightly unhappy constantly.
— J. D. Salinger

"Sure hope you become a writer." That was it. Just those six words. It was the first time someone had indicated in any way that writing was a career option for me.
— Dave Eggars, on being inspired by a school teacher to become a writer

I realized that books could be so engrossing that nothing else mattered. That was the moment I took my first step toward becoming a writer.

— Michael Castleman, on being influenced by his mother's reverence for books

There are only two ways to live: for literature, or as literature.

— Joshua Coen

Being a fiction writer is a nice net to have. I like writing much more than being a writer.

— John Sayles

Novels have more to do with desire—translating desire into prose—and a temperament that accepts concentration over the long haul, meaning the ability to sit alone in one place day by day.

— Ward Just

Writing is a socially acceptable form of schizophrenia.

— E. L. Doctorow, attributed

If you're a singer you lose your voice. A baseball player loses his arm. A writer gets more knowledge, and if he's good, the older he gets, the better he writes.

— Mickey Spillane

You can teach almost anyone determined to learn them the basics required to write sentences and paragraphs that say what you want them to say clearly and concisely. It's far more difficult to get people to think like a writer, to give up conventional habits of mind and emotion.

— Anne Bernays

Either write something worth reading or do something worth writing.

— Benjamin Franklin

With a novel, you are the architect and the builder, the god. When you write the script, you are like the guy who does the flooring.
    — Dennis Lehane, describing the difference between writing a novel and working on a film screenplay

Getting the rhythm [is the hardest part of writing] . . . so much depends on continuity.
    — Ralph Ellison

The book that changed my life—that made me yearn to be a writer as well as inspired me to "write"—is Lewis Carroll's *Alice in Wonderland and Through the Looking Glass*, a combination of the two classics in one volume.

— Joyce Carol Oates

The only good in pretending is the fun we get out of fooling ourselves that we fool somebody.

— Booth Tarkington

A writer never has a vacation. For a writer life consists of either writing or thinking about writing.

— Eugene Ionesco

No man but a blockhead ever wrote except for money.

— Samuel Johnson

Quotation is the highest compliment you can pay to a writer.

— Samuel Johnson

Truth is stranger than fiction; fiction is obliged to stick to possibilities, truth isn't.

— Mark Twain

The first qualification for a historian is to have no ability to invent.

— Stendhal

I seem to have some neurotic need to be perfect, each paragraph—each sentence, even—as I go along.

— William Styron, explaining his transcribing his
writing from his handwritten yellow pads

It may not always be a bad thing for a young writer to emulate a master, even in an obvious way.

— William Styron, describing being influenced by
his admiration of Robert Penn Warren

It is perhaps inevitable that nearly all very good writers seem to be able to inspire the most vehement personal reactions.

— William Styron

It takes years to write a book—between two and ten years. Less is so rare as to be statistically insignificant.

— Annie Dillard

One of the few things I know about writing is this: spend it all, shoot it, play it, lose it, all, right away, every time. Do not hoard what seems good for a later place in the book, or for another book, give it, give it all, give it now.

— Annie Dillard

There may be some writers who contemplate a day's work without dread, but I don't know them.

— Mary Gordon

There is never enough time for writing; it is a parallel universe where the days, inconveniently, are also 24 hours long. Every moment spent in one's real life is a moment missed in one's writing life, and vice versa.

— Gish Gen

One must live in order to have something to write about. That's the common place wisdom, and to be engaged with the world is no bad thing, it is essential.

— Gish Gen

All good writing is swimming under the water and holding your breath.

— F. Scott Fitzgerald

Every writer scrounges for inspiration in different places, and there's no shame in reading the headlines. It's necessary, in fact, when attempting contemporary satire. Sharp-edged humor relies on reference points.

— Carl Hiaasen

The test of a first-rate intelligence is the ability to hold two opposed ideas in the mind at the same time, and still retain the ability to function.

— F. Scott Fitzgerald

Writing is my way of thinking out loud through puzzles that interest me.

— Atul Gawande

Inversion therapy . . . does help. You've just got to relax and let go. The more you do it the more you let go. And then it's just "wow."

— Dan Brown

I am a completely horizontal author. I can't think unless I'm lying down, either in bed or stretched on a couch and with a cigarette and coffee handy. I've got to be puffing and sipping.

— Truman Capote

Well, I think if there's a major theme in my work . . . it is the impact of character upon character, how people rub against one another and alter one another.

— Carolyn Kizer

Writers love distraction. All that crap about going off into the woods and writing all day? I don't buy it. I can't wait for the mailman. Your phone call made my day.

— Robert B. Parker

If you can't annoy somebody, there's little point in writing.

— Kingsley Amis

I am always writing the same book.

— Patrick Modiano

You most likely need a thesaurus, a rudimentary grammar book, and a grip on reality. This latter means: there's no free lunch. Writing is work. It's also gambling. You don't get a pension plan. Other people can help you a bit, but—essentially you're on your own. Nobody is making you do this: you chose it, so don't whine.

— Margaret Atwood

But in the magical world of writing, it is possible for an author to give birth to characters and elements that grow beyond his or her control.

— Anne Rice

Read, read, read. Read everything—trash, classics, good and bad, and see how they do it. Just like a carpenter who works as an apprentice and studies the master.

— William Faulkner, attributed

Each book is like a stepping stone to the next book. It is a very unconscious process. Writing is very unconscious.

— Edna O'Brien

I write only in pen and ink, and I labor over every word. I have made a rule for myself: I don't start until I feel I have my title, my first paragraph, and my last paragraph. I can't choose the ending as I go along. I've got to have that before I begin to write.

— Penelope Fitzgerald

It's that unknown that keeps us going, I think. It's the same thing that drives you to read a book—or write one. That you don't know what's coming on the next page, in the next chapter. An unusual snake. An elusive bird. A crime you'd never considered, with an explanation you didn't see coming.

— Gerry Boyle

Writing is my salvation. If I didn't write, what would I do?

— Maxine Kumin

When you're the writer, you're the captain of the ship and the blank page is the great wide open ocean for all your ideas and visions.

— Nila Webster

A writer is a man who, embarking upon a task, does not know what to do.

— Donald Barthelme

Covering the lines with black slanted letters from the pen connected me with the flow of my life.

— Gail Godwin, giving up typing for a plain pilot pen

Sometimes there's an enormous weight of emotion which you have nowhere to take. I think it's a reason writers drink; you can get so incredibly wound up you're weeping and laughing. Writing is how I justify my existence.

— Robert Stone

I use the white space. I'm interested in precise meaning and in reverberation, in associative levels. What you're trying to do when you write is to crowd the reader out of his own space and occupy it with yours, in a good cause. You're trying to take over his sensibility and deliver an experience that moves from mere information.

— Robert Stone

Everyone needs an editor to save you from yourself.

— Callie Crossley

If ever the facts are presented fairly and honestly, the truth will take care of itself.

— George Seldes

Chapter Two

On Journalism

If ever the facts are presented fairly and honestly, the truth will take care of itself.

— George Seldes

My philosophy is that you have faith in the writer's point of view. You pick the writers you believe in and give them their freedom. As opposed to most editors who want to mold the writers into what they want, make them a tool of the editors.

— Clay Felker, editor

The best charge against bias is accuracy.

— Bob Schieffer

Because Americans have had from the beginning a "free" press, we have had a longer tradition of the congenital nay-sayer, the contrary-minded, and the "come-outer" than most other nations.

— Henry Steele Commager

For a journalist, there is no such thing as useless knowledge. Every act from every discipline has the potential to brighten style or strengthen substance.

— Dick Shaap

Modern journalism, by giving us the opinions of the uneducated, keeps us in touch with the ignorance of the Community.

— Oscar Wilde

Journalism is a profession whose practitioners should know everything and pretend to know nothing. Too many people in the profession know nothing and pretend to know everything.

— Dick Shaap

With his newspapers, which were irresistible reading for twelve-year-olds, he also acquainted me with the existence of "love nests" and the arresting fact that a woman of "statuesque" proportions was often to be found in one, sometimes lying defunct in "a pool of blood."

— Russell Baker, describing working for
William Randolph Hearst

But if for [Lord] Acton there was no worse heresy than that the office sanctifies the holder of it, there is for journalism no credo more sacred than that victory, however seedy, certifies the brilliance of the victor.

— Murray Kempton

Tell the Truth and Run.

— George Seldes

Sports may be the "toy department" of journalism, but it gives you the freedom to play serious games.

— Red Smith, attributed

It's a mistake for politicians to comment on the Press, because they're not going to give honest answers.

— Barney Frank

Journalism is not a profession but a mission. Our newspaper is our party, our ideal, our soul, and our banner which will lead us to victory.

— Benito Mussolini

In America the president reigns for four years, and journalism governs for ever and ever.

— Oscar Wilde

Journalism justifies its own existence by the great Darwinian principle of the survival of the vulgarist.

— Oscar Wilde

One of my stronger journalistic peeves is the use of the phrase "investigative reporter" . . . It is redundant. If a reporter is not investigative, he is not a reporter.

— Dick Shaap

Every reporter inhales skepticism. You interview people and they lie. You face public figures, diligently making notes or taping what is said, and they perform their interviews to fit a calculated script. The truth, alas, is always elusive.

— Pete Hamill

My low opinion of editors was never elevated by being one.

— Dick Shaap

News is a Verb

— Pete Hamill

No bureaucracy likes an independent newspaperman . . . whether capitalist or communist, democratic or authoritarian, every regime does its best to color and control the flow of news in its favor.

— I. F. Stone

He was the best reporter I have known, a short, wiry, black-haired man with piercing eyes behind thick glasses. Izzie Stone had an absolute faith in truth, and he pursued it with an almost religious fervor. If anything could save man from his follies, it was truth.

— Tristram Coffin

A writer without a sense of justice and of injustice would be better off editing the yearbook of a school for exceptional children than writing novels.

— Ernest Hemingway

Newspaper work will not harm a young writer and could help him if he gets out of it in time.

— Ernest Hemingway

A scoop isn't a matter of luck, you work, you dig, you make calls, you grab the discrepancy, the loose thread, and you pull. And you have to have been paying attention in the first place. That's not luck.

— I. F. Stone

Don't get intimate with them or you lose your independence and they'll use you.

— I. F. Stone, advising a reporter about covering officials

[With] more news now than ever before, papers need columnists to give them an identity. People need to know who to cuss.

— Eugene Patterson, editor, *St. Petersburg Times*

Walter Winchell, probably the most influential newspaper columnist of the 20th century, was almost universally feared and despised.

— Alex Beam, columnist

Immortality in a business as ephemeral as daily journalism is nigh-on impossible, but every city has a newspaper guy who will be forever identified with that city. H. L. Mencken in Baltimore, Jimmy Breslin in New York, Mike Royko in Chicago, Herb Caen in San Francisco, [George] Frazier—is that guy for Boston.

— Charles Fountain

A litterateur is not a confectioner, not a dealer in cosmetics, not an entertainer . . . He is just like an ordinary reporter. What would you say if a newspaper reporter, because of his fastidiousness or from a wish to give pleasure to his readers, were to describe only honest mayors, high-minded ladies, and virtuous railroad contractors?

— Anton Chekhov

I think being a liberal, in the true sense, is being nondoctrinaire, nondogmatic, noncommitted to a cause—but examining each case on its merits. Being left of center is another thing; it's a political position.

— Walter Cronkite

[Because] journalists are so conformist and lazy it usually takes years for a politician's reputation to catch up with reality.

— Jack Newfield

Most of the news on television is, unfortunately, whatever the government says is news. It's our job to inform people what really is going on.

— Bill Moyers

The First Amendment was not written in order to protect money-making contests, gossip columns, and stories that end with a recipe. It was written into the Constitution on the supposition that newspapers would play an important salutary role as the watchdog of government.

— Jack Newfield

It didn't faze me, because I realized early on that when you get into the business of putting yourself out on the public chopping block, you have to figure you're going to get chopped at.

— William Kennedy,
on his days as a journalist

James Reston, reflecting on his long and distinguished career as a reporter and commentator on national politics for the *New York Times*, concluded that any respect he deserved was probably attributable to his early experience as a sportswriter.

— George V. Higgins

A newspaper gathers more news by trust than by tricks.

— James Reston

Joe McGinniss wasn't one to let a story tell itself. Whether insisting on the guilt of a murder suspect after seemingly befriending him or moving next door to Sarah Palin's house for a most unauthorized biography, he was unique in his determination to get the most inside information, in how publicly he burned bridges with his subjects, and how memorably he placed himself in the narrative.

— Hillel Ialie

He has an instinct for the jugular, a long memory, a sense of irony and humor, a passion for life, and he knows how to make use of the Dewey Decimal System. Above all, he knows that the important question is always: "For whom?"

— Times Books, on the career of
journalist Murray Kempton

In America the president
reigns for four years, and
journalism governs for
ever and ever.

— Oscar Wilde, "The Soul of Man
Under Socialism"

A true American treasure, Orlean lives an adventure-filled writer's life. In doing so, she's created a definition of journalism that didn't exist before and remains unique to her. One suspects that if she were other-gendered, there would be a name for it, like Gonzo journalism or New Journalism. "Sue Journalism" perhaps.

— Meredith Maran

In journalism, there has always been a tension between getting it first and getting it right.

— Ellen Goodman

You can teach someone who cares to write columns, but you can't teach someone who writes columns to care.

— Ellen Goodman

If I'd written all the truth I know for the past ten years, about 600 people—including me—would be rotting in prison cells from Rio to Seattle today. Absolute truth is a very rare and dangerous commodity in the context of professional journalism.

— Hunter S. Thompson, attributed

They're the only people who are paid for telling the truth. They aren't paid enough. But they are paid. A lot of people are paid not to tell the truth. They get very good money for it.

— Ben Bagdikian, editor

All of broadcast and printed news is pulled by a dominant current into a continuous flow of business conservatism. It has a sufficiently powerful effect to shrink other ideas and news of tax-supported social needs necessary in any self-correcting democracy.

— Ben Bagdikian

Editors decide what reporters do. They decide what gets in. They have ultimate control. A reporter can only control what he or she sees.

— Ben Bagdikian

When reporters go after a story, with the same enthusiasm that businessmen go after money, it usually works out best for everyone in both cases even though the businessman's interest is profit and the journalist's interest is a good story.

— Andy Rooney

No one should be pleased with the news we got of all the people in Washington who tried to bypass our democratic system by acting in the manner of unelected dictators. What we should be pleased with is that we got the news about it.

— Andy Rooney

We have seen in our time that the best writers as they mature become journalists— Sartre, Camus, Mauriac, Hemingway.

— A. J. Liebling

First, if you don't ask, you don't find out; and second, the questions don't do the damage. Only the answers do.

— Sam Donaldson

The time to really question something strongly is when everyone says it's true.

— Sam Donaldson

I think in order to do their job, reporters should keep their distance from the powerful people they cover. I think we should consider ourselves outsiders.

— Sam Donaldson

The press must continue its mission of publishing information that it, and it alone, determines to be in the public interest . . . serving society, not government.

— Ben Bradlee

[White is] one of the few writers of this or any century who has succeeded in transforming the ephemera of journalism into something that demands to be called literature.

— Jonathan Yardley, of E. B. White

Moment that changed my life was being hijacked in 1978. Made me a journalist.

— Katrina vanden Heuvel

It is a fundamental fact about journalism and might even be a rule if it had the attention it deserves—that it is next to impossible to judge any public figure with the proper detachment once you begin calling him by his first name.

— Murray Kempton

We journalists make it a point to know very little about an extremely wide variety of topics; this is how we stay objective.

— Dave Barry

The world's a small place and people are watching; and, you know, somebody disappears, the family knows and their colleagues know, and so eventually, these things do get out.

— Jane Mayer

My time on that ship made me aware that as a journalist I would always be both witness and participant; I learned that I must live a story to write it.

— Ruth Gruber, who escorted refugees fleeing Nazis

As a journalist, you must have honor. You have to go places where you are a stranger, so good manners are also essential.

— Murray Kempton

There is nothing much wrong with American newspapers today except us publishers.

— John Cowles

Today, I've written over 3000. People often ask me the secret to lasting so long in the column-writing business. Sincerity, I tell them. Once you can fake that, you've got it made. Which is typical of people who work for newspapers. We use sarcasm to avoid revealing genuine emotion.

— Roger Simon

Our job is not to amuse our readers. Our mission is to stir them, inform, and inflame them. Our task is to continually hold up our government and our leaders to clear-eyed analysis, unaffected by professional spin-meisters and agenda-pushers.

— Tony Auth, editorial cartoonist

A journalist is stimulated by a deadline; he writes worse when he has time.

— Karl Kraus

Most journalists are restless voyeurs who see the warts on the world, the imperfections on people and places . . . gloom is their game, the spectacle their passion, normality their nemesis.

— Gay Talese

As far as I'm concerned, it's a damned shame that a field as potentially dynamic and vital as journalism should be overrun with dullards, bums, and hacks, hag-ridden with myopia, apathy, and complacence, and generally stuck in a bog of stagnant mediocrity.

— Hunter S. Thompson

The TV business is uglier than most things. It is normally perceived as some kind of cruel and shallow money trench through the heart of the journalism industry, a long plastic hallway where thieves and pimps run free and good men die like dogs, for no good reason.

— Hunter S. Thompson

A good writer should be able to write comedic work that made you laugh, and scary stuff that made you scared, and fantasy or science fiction that imbued you with a sense of wonder, and mainstream journalism that gave you clear and concise information in a way that you wanted it.

— Neil Gaiman

My favorite type of photography—apart from fashion photography—is journalism, which in a way documents something that exists in a very precise moment, that didn't exist in a moment before and will not exist ever again. This has influenced my work a lot—I usually try to make my images look like they just exist, like no effort was put into it.

— Mario Testino

I think journalism is a great way to do public service, to have an impact on your community.

— Bob Schieffer

The courage in journalism is sticking up for the unpopular, not the popular.

— Geraldo Rivera

I still believe that if your aim is to change the world, journalism is a more immediate short-term weapon.

— Tom Stoppard

I don't think a tough question is disrespectful.

— Helen Thomas

In journalism just one fact that is false prejudices the entire work. In contrast, in fiction one single fact that is true gives legitimacy to the entire work. That's the only difference, and it lies in the commitment of the writer. A novelist can do anything he wants so long as he makes people believe in it.

— Gabriel García Márquez

A key purpose of journalism is to provide an adversarial check on those who wield the greatest power by shining a light on what they do in the dark, and informing the public about those acts.

— Glenn Greenwald

Journalism will kill you, but it will keep you alive while you're at it.

— Horace Greeley

The lowest form of popular culture—lack of information, misinformation, disinformation, and a contempt for the truth or the reality of most people's lives—has overrun real journalism. Today, ordinary Americans are being stuffed with garbage.

— Carl Bernstein

Most rock journalism is people who can't write, interviewing people who can't talk, for people who can't read.

— Frank Zappa

You can't ignore politics, no matter how much you'd like to.
— Molly Ivins

All managing editors are vermin.

— H. L. Mencken

News is what someone wants suppressed. Everything else is advertising. The power is to set the agenda. What we print and what we don't print matter a lot.

— Katharine Graham, editor

One thing I learned as a journalist is that there is at least one disgruntled person in every workplace in America—and at least double that number with a conscience. Hard as they try, they simply can't turn their heads away from an injustice when they see one taking place.

— Michael Moore

No writer ever really wants to talk about censorship. Writers want to talk about creation, and censorship is anti-creation, negative energy, uncreation, the bringing into being of non-being, or, to use Tom Stoppard's description of death, "the absence of presence."

— Salman Rushdie

Chapter Three

On Censorship

Censorship is when a person or group successfully imposes their values upon others by stifling words, images or ideas and preventing them from reaching the public marketplace of ideas. From as early as 399 BC, when Socrates was sentenced to drink poison for corrupting his students, to the school board debates over textbooks that occur in contemporary America, attempts to stifle ideas through censorship are a feature of societies, both primitive and advanced.

— LeHigh University project on censorship

The mind is its own cosmos. It can make a heaven of hell or a hell of heaven.

— John Milton

I have sworn . . . eternal hostility against every form of tyranny over the mind of man.

— Thomas Jefferson

We have a natural right to make use of our pens as of our tongue, at our peril, risk and hazard.

— Voltaire

I believe strongly in government support for the arts—believe, in fact, that a government that does not support the arts harms both itself and the nation. I also believe that support is meaningless, even harmful, if it restricts the imaginative freedom of those to whom it is given.

— Wallace Stegner, in refusing the National Medal of the Arts, by the Bush Administration in 1992, because of the political controls put on some artists

We Negro writers, just by being black, have been on the blacklist all our lives. Censorship for us begins at the color line.

— Langston Hughes

Censor: a man who knows more than he thinks you ought to.

— Granville Hicks

Art is on the side of the oppressed. Think before you shudder at the simplistic dictum and its heretical definition of the freedom of art. For if art is freedom of the spirit, how can it exist within the oppressors?

— Nadine Gordimer

I believe you can write about anything. Nothing should be excluded from the world of books; that's what books are for. But I got reviews whose last words were "shut up."

— Kathryn Harrison

No writer ever really wants to talk about censorship. Writers want to talk about creation, and censorship is anti-creation, negative energy, uncreation, the bringing into being of non-being, or, to use Tom Stoppard's description of death, "the absence of presence."

— Salman Rushdie

There is no doubt that Hemingway has sacrificed thousands in his sales by the use of what we have come to call the "four letter" words and I do not think he need have done it.

— Max Perkins

To equate the free and robust exchange of ideas and political debate with commercial exploitation of obscene material demeans the grand conception of the First Amendment and its high purposes in the historic struggle for freedom. It is a misuse of the great guarantee of free speech and free press.

— Chief Justice Warren Burger

And art made tongue-tied by authority

— William Shakespeare

I'm all in favor of keeping dangerous weapons out of the hands of fools. Let's start with typewriters.

— Frank Lloyd Wright

There will always be taboos as long as the powerful are allowed to define what writers are forbidden to write.

— Francine Prose, attributed

Censorship is the thing that stops you doing what you want to do, and what writers want to talk about is what they do, not what stops them doing it.

— Salman Rushdie

If we are not confident of our freedom, then we are not free.

— Salman Rushdie

Drawing a line between state-sponsored censorship and censorship from other sources may seem like making a distinction without a difference, but consider the intensity of graduation speaker controversies today . . . When colleges act this way in a country with a well-functioning civil society, they are reneging on their responsibilities as bastions of free inquiry.

— Nelson L. Barrette

Obscenity can be found in every book except the telephone directory.

— George Bernard Shaw

Censorship ends in logical completeness when nobody is allowed to read any books except the books nobody can read.

— George Bernard Shaw

Art made tongue-tied by authority.

— William Shakespeare

It seems to me we were all better off when the Postal Department used to deliver the mail and left it to a Higher Authority to deliver us from evil.

— Herbert L. Block

Provided I do not write about the government, religion, politics, morals, people in power, official institutions, the Opera, the other theatres, or about anybody attached to anything, I am free to print anything, subject to the inspection of two or three censors.

— Pierre-Augustin de Beaumarchais

Let people talk, let them blame you, condemn you, imprison you, even hang you, but publish what you think. It is not a right, but a duty, a strict obligation laid upon anyone who thinks, to express what he thinks in public for the common good ... To speak is a good thing, to write it better, to print, an excellent thing.

— Paul-Louis Courier

Certain members of your community have suggested that my work is evil. This is extraordinarily insulting to me. The news from Drake indicates to me that books and writers are very unreal to you people. I am writing this letter to let you know how real I am.

— Kurt Vonnegut, responding to a school committee
that banned his books

To hear that the novel is "immoral" has made me count the years between now and 1984, for I have yet to come across a better example of doublethink.

— Harper Lee, upon learning from a local school board
that *To Kill a Mockingbird* was banned

It has enormous repercussions. It makes one, or did to me at the time, feel secretly that I must have done something wrong, that there was some criminality in what I did.

— Edna O'Brien, on her work being banned

Submitting to censorship is to enter the seductive world of *The Giver:* the world where there are no bad words and no bad deeds. But it is also the world where choice has been taken away and reality distorted. And that is the most dangerous world of all.

— Lois Lowry

There is a fine line between censorship and good taste and moral responsibility.

— Stephen Spielberg

Censorship is to art as lynching is to justice.

— Henry Louis Gates

In all my life, I have never been free. I have never been able to do anything with freedom, except in the field of my writing.

— Langston Hughes

Censorship reflects a society's lack of confidence in itself.

— Potter Stewart

Let children read whatever they want and then talk about it with them. If parents and kids can talk together, we won't have as much censorship because we won't have as much fear.

— Judy Blume

We live in oppressive times. We have, as a nation, become our own thought police; but instead of calling the process by which we limit our expression of dissent and wonder "censorship," we call it "concern for commercial viability."

— David Mamet

Dubliners—was ripped up, burned, bowdlerized, rejected, resurrected, lost, dismissed, forgotten, thrown away, flogged, flayed and eventually celebrated.

— Colum McCann

Ulysses is the most important contribution that has been made to fictional literature in the twentieth century.

— Dr. Joseph Collins

One cannot and must not try to erase the past merely because it does not fit the present.

— Golda Meir

Here's the rub: If I wrote novels for adults and someone took umbrage at what I'd written they'd call me "distasteful," maybe "offensive." But as a writer for children and teenagers, I get accused of "corrupting" the readers. It's a strong and worrying distinction.

— Keith Gessen

These bannings don't seem to be due to offensive language or the subject of sex itself, but because the book doesn't conform to a particular worldview or philosophy. Do these schools only want their students to read approved, sanctioned, authorized books? Unfortunately it seems they do. But approved by whom? Authorized by whom?

— Keith Gessen

Censors try to limit the freedom of others to choose what they read, see, or hear. Sex, profanity, and racism remain the primary categories of objections, and most occur in schools and school libraries. Frequently, challenges are motivated by the desire to protect children.

— Robert P. Doyle

When it comes to the written word, censorship debates are no longer about taste and decency—although those issues are much in the news concerning the visual arts, television and radio. Instead, the debate over books tends to center on geopolitics, national security and foreign policy.

— Rachel Donadio

Even if the Patriot Act itself is not directly censorious, if it causes someone to censor herself at the library for fear of the government finding out she is interested in Islam, if it stops someone from buying a book about terrorism because someone might be watching, then the Patriot Act is censorship.

— Stefanie, *So Many Books* blog

Most teachers and librarians won't acknowledge [that they self-censor], so we don't know how deep or widespread [censoring] is . . . Talking to teachers and school librarians, they do self-censor.

— Nat Hentoff

If I were teaching journalism at a high school, graduate school, or in a newsroom, I would cite what Voice of America's then-acting director, Myrna Whitworth, told the staff, urging it "NOT to fall under the spell of 'self-censorship.' If you do, 'they' have won . . . Continue to interview anyone, anywhere.

— Nat Hentoff

Without freedom of thought, there can be no such thing as wisdom; and no such thing as public liberty, without freedom of speech.

— Benjamin Franklin

It's not just the books under fire now that worry me. It is the books that will never be written. The books that will never be read. And all due to the fear of censorship. As always, young readers will be the real losers.

— Judy Blume

Censorship ends in logical completeness when nobody is allowed to read any books except the books nobody can read.

— George Bernard Shaw

Restriction of free thought and free speech is the most dangerous of all subversions. It is the one un-American act that could most easily defeat us.

— William O. Douglas

Many parents confuse a book's subject matter with the notion that the author or publisher advocates a particular moral agenda and have come to regard books as enemies. For example, a book that contains profanity may be seen as one that encourages kids to use bad language. Or a book that portrays a rebellious child is seen as urging children toward anti-family behavior.

— Suzanne Fisher Staples

And on the subject of burning books: I want to congratulate librarians, not famous for their physical strength or their powerful political connections or their great wealth, who, all over this country, have staunchly resisted antidemocratic bullies who have tried to remove certain books from their shelves, and have refused to reveal to thought police the names of persons who have checked out those titles. So the America I loved still exists, if not in the White House or the Supreme Court or the Senate or the House of Representatives or the media. The America I love still exists at the front desks of our public libraries.

— Kurt Vonnegut

Censorship is the tool of those who have the need to hide actualities from themselves and from others. Their fear is only their inability to face what is real, and I can't vent any anger against them. I only feel this appalling sadness. Somewhere, in their upbringing, they were shielded against the total facts of our existence. They were only taught to look one way when many ways exist.

— Charles Bukowski

I think that the role of an educator is to encourage critical thinking and debate, and that this is a . . . way to address "controversial" material in schools.

— Cory Doctorow

For a citizen in our free society, it is an enormous privilege and a wonderful protection to have access to hundreds of periodicals, each peddling its own belief. There is safety in numbers: the papers expose each other's follies and peccadillos, correct each other's mistakes, and cancel out each other's biases. The reader is free to range around in the whole editorial bouillabaisse and explore it for the one clam that matters—the truth.

— E. B. White

It's okay to be offensive. That's what free speech is all about. If free speech is only what you like, it's not free speech.

— Sen. Angus King

The important task of literature is to free man, not to censor him, and that is why Puritanism was the most destructive and evil force which ever oppressed people and their literature: it created hypocrisy, perversion, fears, sterility.

— Anaïs Nin

Say anything, don't censor your mind, don't censor your language.

— Philip Roth

In 2006 some parents in a Kansas school district decided that talking animals are blasphemous and unnatural; passages about the spider dying were also criticized as being "inappropriate subject matter for a children's book." According to the parent group at the heart of the issue, "humans are the highest level of God's creation and are the only creatures that can communicate vocally. Showing lower life forms with human abilities is sacrilegious and disrespectful to God."

— Banned Books Awareness org. on
the banning of *Charlotte's Web* by E. B. White

Consider what would happen if—during the 200th anniversary of the Bill of Rights—the First Amendment were placed on the ballot in every town, city and state. The choices: affirm, reject, or amend. I would bet there is no place in the United States where the First Amendment would survive intact.

— Nat Hentoff

Every time you take a book out of a library you deny someone that particular voice.

— Sarah Dessen

Many a time freedom has been rolled back—and always for the same sorry reason: fear.

— Molly Ivins

And who is to decide. Well keep that question if you would . . . every time you silence someone you make yourself a prisoner of your own action because you deny yourself the right to hear something.

— Christopher Hitchens

All these people talk so eloquently about getting back to good old-fashioned values . . . and I say let's get back to the good old-fashioned First Amendment of the good old-fashioned Constitution of the United States—and to hell with the censors! Give me knowledge or give me death!

— Kurt Vonnegut

Poetry is the rhythmical creation of beauty in words.

— Edgar Allan Poe

Chapter Four

On Poetry

Poetry: The art of rhythmical composition, written or spoken, for exciting pleasure by beautiful, imaginative, or elevated thoughts.

— Dictionary.com

Suicide is, after all, the opposite of the poem.

— Anne Sexton

The poem's loveliness resides in the sounds it makes and in the pictures it evokes. One can respond to it as a piece of music—without concern for meaning. This is not to say that the poem is without meaning, rather, it is a reminder that poetry functions as more than an occasion for analysis.

— Robert B. Parker

Biographers try to figure out why poets write the way they do—which leads to lots of explanation and equivocation, not many answers.

— Daisy Fried

Poetry, even in the same act and the same moment, helps one to grasp reality and to grasp one's own life. Not that it will give definitions and certainties.

— Robert Penn Warren

The progress of an artist is a continual self-sacrifice, a continual extinction of personality. Honest criticism and sensitive appreciation is directed not upon the poet but upon the poetry.

— T. S. Eliot

Poetry is an explanation; the process of writing is an exploration. You may dimly envisage what a poem will be when you start it, but only as you wrangle through the process do you know your own meanings.

— Robert Penn Warren

The armored cars of dreams contrived to let us do so many a dangerous thing.

— Elizabeth Bishop

The poem is a way of knowing what kind of a person you can be, getting your reality shaped a little bit better.

— Robert Penn Warren

We do not read poetry so that we can write better memoranda later on. We want instead fully realized human beings who will read poetry because it is beautiful and because it brings us knowledge of what is true, even if it is knowledge that can no more be used than a sunset or a kiss can be used.

— The Pioneer Institute, the Boston think tank lamenting a change in curriculum standards de-emphasizing poetry

The immature poet imitates, the mature poet plagiarizes.

— T. S. Eliot, attributed

It is instilled in the American poet at a very early age that something is anti-poetic in the state of America.

— Karl Shapiro

Poetry is the opening and closing of a door, leaving those who look through it to guess about what is seen during a moment.

— Carl Sandburg

In a way, poetry far outlasts politics. Poetry transcends time.

— Eric Anderson

To see and hear Berryman lecture on a text he loved was to be in the presence of the transcendent. To describe it otherwise would be imprecise and he was ever for precision.

— Janet Groth

Poetry is the rhythmical creation of beauty in words.

— Edgar Allan Poe

Poets are much more concerned with arranging images than with creating them.

— Victor Shklovsky

More than anyone else, I suppose, Dylan reminds me of an American Brecht—the Brecht whose poems were meant to be sung.

— John Clellon Holmes

Now comes the public and demands that we explain what the poet is trying to stay. The answer is this: If we knew exactly he would not be a poet.

— Hermann Bahr

Poetry is when an emotion has found its thought and the thought has found words.

— Robert Frost

All of Greek literature really grows out of Homer.

— I. F. Stone

Our human life is distinguished from other life by language. Poetry is the ancient artistic form of language, our distinction.

— Allen Grossman

Writing free verse is like playing tennis with the net down.

— Robert Frost

There is no money in poetry, but then there is no poetry in money, either.

— Robert Graves

A publisher today would as soon see a burglar in his office as a poet.

— Henry Stackpole

Poetry, for Salinger, represented communion with God.

— Joanna Rakoff

There are two ways of disliking poetry: one way is to dislike it, the other is to read Pope.

— Oscar Wilde

"Howl" is meant to be a noun, but I can't help taking it as an imperative.

— John Hollander, on "Howl" by Allen Ginsberg

Poetry is a deal of joy and pain and wonder, with a dash of the dictionary.

— Kahlil Gibran

Poets live the lives all of us live, with one big difference. They have the power . . . to create a world of thoughts and emotions others can share.

— Bill Moyers

Poetry—is the language in which man explores his own amazement.

— Christopher Fry

A poem is a kind of miracle of words. It can tell a story, flash scenes and images to the mind's eye, and use many fewer words than any other kind of writing.

— Barbara Rogasky

Poets—are born, not paid.

— Addison Mizner

The subject is a fascinating
one. I think poetry is the
greatest of the arts. It combines
music and painting and story-
telling and prophecy and the
dance. It is religious in tone,
scientific in attitude.

— E. B. White

A poet is one who feels the world as a gift.

— James Dickey

A poet's pleasure is to withhold a little of his meaning, to intensify by mystification. He unzips the veil from beauty but does not remove it. A poet utterly clear is a trifle glaring.

— E. B. White

The subject is a fascinating one. I think poetry is the greatest of the arts. It combines music and painting and story-telling and prophecy and the dance. It is religious in tone, scientific in attitude.

— E. B. White

Poetry is when an emotion has found its thought and the thought has found words.

— Robert Frost

Genuine poetry can communicate before it is understood.

— T. S. Eliot

If I read a book and it makes my whole body so cold no fire can ever warm me, I know that is poetry.

— Emily Dickinson

Writing poetry is an unnatural act. It takes skill to make it seem natural.

— Elizabeth Bishop

Throw away the light, the definitions, and say what you see in the dark.
— Wallace Stevens, attributed

Everything in art is connected. Every single moment is the past, the present, and the future.

— Richard Blanco

The harder—that is, the more psychically difficult—the poem is to write, the more likely I am to choose a difficult pattern to pound it into. This is true because, paradoxically, the difficulty frees me to be more honest and more direct.

— Maxine Kumin

It's the poet's job to figure out what's happening within oneself, to figure out the connection between the self and the world, and to get it down in words that have a certain shape, that have a chance of lasting.

— Galway Kinnell

I'm a great believer in poetry out of the classroom, in public places, on subways, trains, on cocktail napkins. I'd rather have my poems on the subway than around the seminar table at an MFA program.

— Billy Collins

Leaving out the talking points and underselling meanings, a poem is not an argument. It's a challenge. And the challenge is to examine the evidence of the world. Often trying to look at things from another's perspective, or just from her own viewpoint of practiced attention, the poet has seen something, and she wants you to look at it, too. Real looking leads to real seeing, it literally makes you think.

— Mike Corrigan

If I feel physically as if the top of my head were taken off, I know that is poetry.

— Emily Dickinson

Every day you play with the light of the universe.

— Pablo Neruda

Poetry will save nothing from oblivion, but I keep writing about the ordinary because for me it's the home of the extraordinary, the only home.

— Philip Levine

I don't know. I really don't know. I know why it matters to me. I can't speak for anyone else. It changed my life. It gave me some valve for the emotional longings that I had as a young man and helped me bring together various independent thoughts that I had. It was very important to me, and I always had a love of language, which is the first thing you have to have if you want to write poems. You've got to love the language.

— Charles Wright, when asked if poetry matters

I'm a line-maker. I think that's what makes poets different from prose-writers. That's the main way. We think, not just in sentences the way prose writers do but also in lines. So we're doing these two things at the same time.

— Billy Collins

You can have the other words—chance, luck, coincidence, serendipity. I'll take grace. I don't know what it is exactly, but I'll take it.

— Mary Oliver

Poetry is a life-cherishing force. For poems are not words, after all, but fires for the cold, ropes let down to the lost, something as necessary as bread in the pockets of the hungry.

— Mary Oliver

A poet with the laurels of the people for the people, a minstrel, a speaker, a clown and philosopher, an inspirer, a listener and gatherer, a messenger and a anthropoet, lyrical documenter, a defender of people's expressive rights, a mountain walker and mountain friend, a sun-paddler, a reed of rain, a samba apprentice, a visitor in all homes and terrains, a yes-person to the inner smile of all.

> — Juan Felipe Herrera, asked what is a poet laureate?
> And what are the duties of one?

Don't use the phone. People are never ready to answer it. Use poetry.

> — Jack Kerouac

Perhaps the mission of an artist is to interpret beauty to people—the beauty within themselves.

> — Langston Hughes

I love rhymes; I love to write a poem about New York and rhyme "oysters" with "The Cloisters." And "The lady from Knoxville who bought her brassieres by the boxful." I just feel a sort of small triumph.

> — Garrison Keillor

The best way in the world for breaking a writer's block is to write a lot. Jabbering away on paper, one gets tricked into feeling interested, all at once, in something one is saying, and behold, the magic waters are flowing again.

— John Gardner

Chapter Five

Writer's Block

A usually temporary condition in which a writer finds it impossible to proceed with the writing of a novel, play, or other work.

— Dictionary.com

Writing in my experience, consists of long periods of hanging out, punctuated by the fugue of remorse at the loss of one's powers, and wonder at occasional output in spite of that loss.

— David Mamet

I never showed any more stories to my father. This is known as writer's block.

— William Kennedy

It's when you discover that there's something else going on in your head, when you find the right metaphor, or symbol, or whatever it is you're groping for—and suddenly the work begins to blossom in directions that you couldn't possibly conceive of before then.

— William Kennedy

You can't predict how long it will last. You wait and see.

— Robert Penn Warren

Writer's block? I've never heard of a plumber complain about plumber's block.

— Robert B. Parker

Writer's block is a subject I've given a lot of thought to, since I come up against it so often. I used to try to power through, overriding the block by sheer force of will. Now I look at it differently. I see writer's block as a message from Shadow, informing me that I'm off track. The "block" is the by-product of a faulty choice I've made.

— Sue Grafton

When I come up against writer's block, I go back and read the journals from the early stages of the writing. As odd as this sounds, more than once I've solved a problem and tagged the solution long before I began the actual writing.

— Sue Grafton

Writing in my experience, consists of long periods of hanging out, punctuated by the fugue of remorse at the loss of one's powers, and wonder at occasional output in spite of that loss.

— David Mamet

When I'm looking for an idea, I'll do anything—clean the closet, mow the lawn, work in the garden.

— Kevin Henkes, attributed

Every time I start a book I have to put my horseshoe down and arrange my stones within it until it feels right. And then I don't touch them again until I finish the book. If I feel the need to rearrange the rocks while I'm writing, that's a symptom of a pretty bad block.

— Sara Gruen

It's never that I have writer's block; it's more that I lack the energy for the project, because the energy required is so great. And I know that the social cost to the family is pretty high. I'm here, but I'm mentally not here. I check out and check in.

— Michael Lewis

I think writer's block is simply the dread that you are going to write something horrible. But as a writer, I believe as you sit down at the keys long enough, sooner or later something will come out.

— Roy Blount Jr., attributed

If you want to be a writer, write . . . Save everything you write. If you feel blocked, write through it until you feel your creative juices flowing again. Write.

— Anne Rice

There never has been an American literary life like Henry Roth's and doubtless never will be again . . . and the idea that a writer could overcome a 60-year writer's block was astounding.

— David Mehegan

Of course.

— Russell Banks, when asked if he suffered a writer's block

There's no writer's block; there's only distraction.

— Carolyn Chute

There's no such thing as writer's block. That was invented by people in California who couldn't write.

— Terry Pratchett

Writer's block, I just drove around it four times. All my favorite writers live there.

— Jarod Kintz

I've always said "Writer's Block" is a myth. There is no such thing as writer's block, only writers trying to force something that isn't ready yet.

— Julie Ann Dawson

Writer's block comes from the feeling that one is doing the wrong thing or doing the right thing badly. Fiction written for the wrong reason may fail to satisfy the motive behind it and thus may block the writer, as I've said; but there is no wrong motive for writing fiction.

— John Gardner

The best way in the world for breaking a writer's block is to write a lot. Jabbering away on paper, one gets tricked into feeling interested, all at once, in something one is saying, and behold, the magic waters are flowing again.

— John Gardner

I don't believe in writer's block. Writer's block is when you're running down an alley and all of a sudden you're trapped by a brick wall . . . You see, the problem is that you went down the wrong alley.

— Barry Lyga

Step away from whatever you're writing and do anything that's creative. Paint pictures, write poetry, design images in Photoshop, make a scrapbook or collage, or if you're masculine, build something in the garage . . . The key is to keep exercising the creative part of your brain and eventually you'll tap back into the flow of writing.

— Chuck Sambuchino

Could there be anything worse than Dashiell Hammett's three decades of writer's block?

— Stacy Schiff

Is this the little woman who made this great war?

— Abraham Lincoln, upon meeting
Harriet Beecher Stowe, 1862

Chapter Six

Writers on Writers & the Critics

Writers really take their worst shellacking from other writers . . .

— E. B. White

There is only one thing worse than a bad review, being ignored altogether.

— Theodore White

To escape criticism, do nothing, say nothing, be nothing.

— Elbert Hubbard

For me, writing a negative review feels like being the child in Hans Christian Anderson's "The Emperor's New Clothes."

— Francine Prose

All the faults of the age come from Christianity and Journalism.

— Frank Harris

Literature is news that stays news.

— Ezra Pound

Writers . . . as a class have distinguished themselves as barroom brawlers, drawing-room wolves, breakers of engagements, defaulters of debts, and suicidal maniacs.

— Malcolm Cowley

He . . . decided on his life work: to be the native American Voltaire, the enemy of all puritans, the heretic in the Sunday school, the one-man demolition crew of the genteel tradition, the unregenerate neighborhood brat who stretches a string in the alley to trip the bourgeoisie on its pious homeward journey.

— Alistair Cooke, of H. L. Mencken

Honey, we'll just have to sink to their level.

— Grace Paley to Alice Hoffman at a reading, when asked what to do if the audience started heckling at their reading

He proved in his art and his life that a tabloid man could have the guts of a burglar and the grace of a saint.

— Pete Hamill, of Murray Kempton

The writers who have nothing to say are the ones who you can buy; the others have too high a price.

— Walter Lippmann

All modern American literature comes from one book by Mark Twain called *Huckleberry Finn* **. . . All American writing comes from that. There was nothing before. There has been nothing as good since.**

— Ernest Hemingway

When the day came that *Gatsby* opened its mysteries to me, I felt I'd been awarded a national treasure—what may be the subtlest and most insightful work of literature that ever took this remarkable notion as its subject.

— Robert Stone

She tells me, once, that she became a writer in part because she wanted to know writers.

— Daniel Menaker, referring to Renata Adler

No one describes things like John Updike. I call him the "Great Noticer."

— David Remnick

Though by no means an ordinary man, through literary prestidigitation E. B. White managed to make his inner self seem much like anyone else's—an act that is itself endearing, even though in his case it was not intended to be.

— William Maxwell

I have always been aware that I am by nature self-absorbed and egotistical; to write of myself to the extent that I have done indicates a too great attention to my own life, not enough to the lives of others.

— E. B. White

[Doris] Lessing has never been a great stylist—she writes too fast and prunes too lightly for that.

— J. M. Coetzee

Oh Christ, I couldn't care less.

— Doris Lessing, upon learning she was awarded the Nobel Prize for Literature

I'm sure I've said this before but I'll say it again—there's a kind of problem between critics and writers. A writer falls in love with an idea and gets carried away. A critic looks at the finished product and ignores the rush of a river that went into the writing, which has nothing to do with the kind of temperate thoughts you have about it.

— Doris Lessing

Humanity could be divided into three classes: men, women, and Margaret Fuller.

— Edgar Allan Poe

Is this the little woman who made this great war?

— Abraham Lincoln, upon meeting Harriet Beecher Stowe

"Ah, he is a wag!—and nothing more.

— Henry Wadsworth Longfellow, of Mark Twain

People make a mistake when they confuse a writer with a performer.

— S. J. Perelman

Metalious's writing is mostly undemanding, but it's also, often . . . not bad. Compared to Jacqueline Susann, her 1960s successor, she reads like Willa Cather.

— Thomas Mallon, describing the writing of Grace Metalious's *Peyton Place*

I want to leave a great literary legacy. I will have legal documents so no can ever co-opt my characters or write an Ellroy knockoff book, like when Robert B. Parker finished a Raymond Chandler novel.

— James Ellroy

That's not writing, that's typing.

— Truman Capote, appraising Jack Kerouac's work

Literature is, perhaps, the most powerful of the arts.

— James T. Farrell

Her powers of devastation are ineffable, her repudiation of repose absolutely tragic, and she was never more brilliant and able and interesting.

— Henry James, describing his friend, Edith Wharton

I'm very proud to be your publisher, Miss Stein, but as I've always told you, I don't understand very much of what you're saying.

— Bennett Cerf, to Gertrude Stein in a radio interview

Gay Talese is the most important non-fiction writer of his generation.

— David Halberstam

Classic. A book which people praise and don't read.

— Mark Twain

I am not a Jewish writer, I am a writer who is a Jew.

— Philip Roth

I think that we all ought to get down on our knees every night and thank God for Faulkner. He is the master; he taught us all to observe our own world, the benefits of observing it closely.

— Peter Taylor

I would also point out that even though these stories were written in a spirit of complete and utter malice, not the noxious, downbeat variety. By this I mean that although on an intellectual level I despise most of the people that I write about, just as I despise most of the awful movies that they appear in, I do not despise the movie industry per se.

— Joe Queenan

Hammett was the first American writer to use the detective story for the purposes of a major novelist, to present a vision, blazing if disenchanted, of our lives.

— Ross MacDonald

And of all [Philip] Roth's recent novels, it ventures farthest into the unknowable. In his unshowy way, with all his quotidian specificity and merciless skepticism, Roth is attempting to storm heaven— an endeavor all the more desperately daring because he seems dead certain it's not there.

— David Gates, in a review of *Indignation*

Once again, words fail Norman Mailer.

—Gore Vidal, after being punched by Mailer after a review

Classic. A book which people praise and don't read.

— Mark Twain

Here I am scribbling away, a thousand percent conscious that writers such as Didion or the columnist Michael Kinsley are out there plying my trade better that I could ever hope to . . . and that's why I love to write, comfortable in the knowledge that there is a glorious universe of talent superior to mine. I hear their music, and it inspires me.

— Alex Beam

Ernest Hemingway was the first major American writer to discover the value of sports as a metaphor for life.

— Robert B. Parker

Updike has produced one of the worst pieces of writing from any grown-up source since the events he has so unwisely tried to draw upon.

— Christopher Hitchens, in a review of
John Updike's *Terrorist*

Every thought you now have and every act and intention owes its complexion to the acts of your dead and living brothers.

— William James

A kind of brilliant actionlessness . . . The world is all metaphor.

— Alfred Kazin, of John Updike

I read Michael Lewis for the same reason I watch Tiger Woods. I'll never play like that. But it's good to be reminded every now and again what genius looks like.

— Malcolm Gladwell

He was a demanding worker. He rewrote the first page of *Charlotte's Web* eight times, and put the early manuscript away for several months "to let the heat out of it."

— Roger Angell, of E. B. White

Gunter Grass is simply the most original and versatile writer alive.

— Saturday Review

The first piece of literature since the Book of Genesis that should be required reading for the entire human race.

— William Kennedy on the novel,
One Hundred Years of Solitude,
by Gabriel García Márquez

He amuses; he frightens; he flirts with doom. His achievement is substantial.

— Garry Wills, of Hunter S. Thompson

He has a remarkable ability to see the human virtues in those who are ideological enemies and moral pariahs to conventional liberals.

— Ron Rosenbaum, on his admiration for
writer/journalist Murray Kempton

It would be fair to say that his books are philosophical romances and that Warren is thereby the true heir to Hawthorne and Melville.

— J. D. McClatchy, of Robert Penn Warren

I was in my early 20s when I read it and it hit me very hard. I re-read it many times.

— Robert Penn Warren, on *An American Tragedy*
by Theodore Dreiser

For all the enormous seriousness of his craft, Bill Shirer had a saving grace that kept him going despite decades of the journalist's vices— bad hours, bad cigarettes, good whiskey and fair coffee. The man had a quizzical sense of humor about the human condition.

— M. R. Montgomery

The most important English practitioner [of the short story].

— Elizabeth Bowen, of V. S. Pritchett

If Robert Crichton walked down to the drug store to buy a cigar, when he returned to tell of the trip it would sound like Homer's "Odyssey."

— Webster Schott

I never said that about any other writer. He was the best critic in the English language.

— Gore Vidal, praising V. S. Pritchett

Erasmus traveled with 32 volumes, which contained all the knowledge worth knowing. Susan Sontag carries it in her brain.

— Carlos Fuentes

Now, Dreiser is an old passion. I've read all of Dreiser and have had many different opinions of him along the way. Humanly he was a monster.

— Robert Penn Warren

For the past 30 years the greatest novelists writing in English have been genre writers: John le Carré, George Higgins and Patrick O'Brian.

— David Mamet

Meg Wolitzer is an author who makes you wonder why more people don't write perceptive, entertaining, unassuming novels about how and why ordinary people choose to make decisions about their lives.

— Nick Hornby

Our greatest living man of letters.

— *Boston Globe*, of Gore Vidal

When he died, at seventy-seven, he was busy stuffing his head with irregular Hungarian verbs. Plainly, he had a brain to match his liver.

— Gore Vidal, of critic Edmund Wilson

I write to make art and change society. That I do either is certainly arguable, but money is not an interest.

— Gore Vidal

The extraordinary worldwide attention paid to the death of Gabriel García Márquez, and the genuine sorrow felt by readers everywhere at his passing, tell us that books are still very much alive.

— Salman Rushdie

When you're a columnist there are days you have nothing to say, and it shows. When you're a critic, your subject is always right in front of you.

— Jay Carr, film critic, *Boston Globe*

He has that surprisingly rare quality in an editor. He makes you want to write.

— Renata Adler, of *New York Times* editor Arthur Gelb

A critic is someone who enters the battlefield after the war is over and shoots the wounded.

— Murray Kempton

I once asked Gunter Grass . . . should writers go into politics? He turned a silent glare upon me, as if it outraged him — to be seated beside a village idiot.

— Saul Bellow

Every word she writes is a lie, including "and" and "the."

— Mary McCarthy, of Lillian Hellman

You can't, by just leading your daily life, really see a goddamn thing. You have to force yourself to get into unfamiliar areas.

— Tom Wolfe, of J. D. Salinger

The only reason I hope I predecease him is that I'd find it next to impossible to say anything nice about him at his memorial service.

— Philip Larkin, of Kingsley Amis

Princess Daisy is a terrible book only in the sense that it is almost totally inept.

— Clive James, of Judith Krantz

Upset by a poor review, he named one of the villains in his next novel after [his critic].

— Joseph P. Kahn, of Joseph Finder

Better than anyone else, he told the truth about his time, the first half of the twentieth century. He was a professional. He wrote honestly and well.

> — The epitaph of John O'Hara, which he wrote himself

In the opinion of many—the finest writer on *The New Yorker* is Joseph Mitchell.

> — Brendan Gill

John Cheever wrote some of his early stories in his underwear . . . Thomas Wolfe reportedly wrote parts of his voluminous novels while leaning over the top of a refrigerator. Flannery O'Connor sat for two hours every day at a typewriter facing the back of a clothes dresser.

> — Kent Haruf

Kipling strikes me personally as the most complete man of genius (as distinct from fine intelligence) that I have ever known.

> — Henry James

In a properly run culture, Mary Frances Kennedy Fisher would be recognized as one of the great writers this country has produced in this century.

> — Raymond Sokolov, of food writer M. F. K. Fisher

Whenever I write a review of a book, it must be to celebrate. Why should I be the one to mete out punishment to a writer or to an artist or to a poet?

— Elie Wiesel

The only war novel I've read that makes any sense.

— Harper Lee, on Joseph Heller's *Catch-22*

Among his peers at *The New Yorker*, Joseph Mitchell was the most admired writer of fact in the magazine's history.

— Janet Groth, author and receptionist at *The New Yorker*

He knew the only honest way to write about love.

—Thomas Pynchon
of Gabriel García Márquez, attributed

[He] is the most perfect writer of my generation, he writes the best sentences word for word, rhythm upon rhythm.

— Norman Mailer, of Truman Capote

Kipling strikes me personally as the most complete man of genius (as distinct from fine intelligence) that I have ever known.

— Henry James

As a short story writer, he has had few equals in the second half of the twentieth century.

> — Gore Vidal, of Paul Bowles

One of the best crime fiction writers in America today.

> — Nelson DeMille, of Linda Fairstein

May Sarton will never be considered a great writer. But she is that rare phenomenon, an appealing writer whose work has the power to change readers' lives.

> — Margot Peters

[One of] the great achievements in American writing this century.

> — Walter Allen, on the novel, *Call It Sleep*, by Henry Roth

I think he is a better and more original writer than Steinbeck, for example, and will last longer.

> — Ross Macdonald, of Dashiell Hammett

He wrote scenes that seemed never to have been written before.

— Raymond Chandler, of Dashiell Hammett

Wilson is one of the most intellectual Americans writing, but he sounds like a smarty-pants when he writes fiction.

— Max Perkins, of Edmund Wilson

If [writers] believe the critics when they say they are great then they must believe them when they say they are rotten and they lose confidence.

— Ernest Hemingway

Editors are extremely fallible people, all of them. Don't put too must trust in them.

— Max Perkins

He'll deny that he pays any attention to what's written about him, but he'll read the stuff like a hawk.

— Elizabeth Thompson and David Gutman,
of Bob Dylan

Humor is a by-product that occurs in the serious work of some and not others. I was more influenced by Don Marquis than by Ernest Hemingway, by Perelman than by Dreiser.

— E. B. White, attributed

Some time ago a publisher told me that there are four kinds of books that seldom, if ever, lose money in the United States—first, murder stories; secondly, novels in which the heroine is forcibly overcome by the hero; thirdly, volumes on spiritualism, occultism and other such claptrap, and fourthly, books on Lincoln.

— H. L. Mencken

Without question the bravest and most original, if perhaps also the least orderly and judicious, of the critics that we have produced.

— H. L. Mencken, of Edgar Allan Poe

This incredible work is an almost inexhaustible mine of bad writing, faulty generalizing, childish pussyfooting, ludicrous posturing, and naive stupidity. To find a match for it one must try to imagine a biography of the Duke of Wellington by his barber.

— H. L. Mencken, on *The New Freedom*,
by Dr. William Bayard Hale

Whoever it was who translated the Bible into excellent French prose is chiefly responsible for the collapse of Christianity in France.

— H. L. Mencken

A reader's heart must go out to a young writer with a sense of wonder so fearless and unbridled. It is this intensity of experience that she seems to live in order to declare.

— Eudora Welty, on Annie Dillard's *Pilgrim at Tinker Creek*

He is very critical of all religions . . . He considers religion as the scourge of humanity.

— The Nobel Swedish Academy, on Nobel Laureate V. S. Naipal

No one in his right mind wants to read Hemingway for pleasure, or Galsworthy.

— V. S. Naipal

A few reviewers have whacked me because I have the temerity to be pleased with myself. They don't like my sense of self-satisfaction; they want me to be a New York intellectual, to be glum and profound.

— Joseph Heller

In the years to come, there will be a Twitter novel, which will be collectible—the question is—how will you collect it?

— Jeremy Dibbell

You'd have to be a masochist to spend years writing the kind of novel you wouldn't enjoy reading yourself.

— James Wolcott

The man has brought more honor to newspapers than anyone in my lifetime.

— Jimmy Breslin, of Murray Kempton

I stole all my stuff on Eisenhower from Murray.

— Historian Garry Wills

Carl loved the midnight glitter. Bob loved the midnight oil.

— Washington Post editor, Ben Bradlee, describing the careers of his reporters, Carl Bernstein and Bob Woodward

Asking a working writer what he thinks about critics is like asking a lamppost how it feels about dogs.

— John Osborne

Be careful about reading health books. You may die of a misprint.

— Mark Twain

Just as jazz and rock-and-roll built a national art form from material dismissed as junk, the Western and then the hard boiled detective story assumed its critical place alongside Shakespeare, Dickens, and Tolstoy, and they did it by way of dime novels and pulp magazines that were cheap enough to read and throw away—but not to forget.

— Loren Estleman

Hammett elevated the private eye story to the status of serious literature.

— Otto Penzler, publisher

Once you've put one of his books down, you simply can't pick it up again.

— Mark Twain, of Henry James, attributed

Criticism is very rarely inhibited by ignorance.

— Mark Twain

Salinger's stories, to a one, are anatomies of loss every inch of them, from start to the finish.

— Joanna Rakoff

A very good library could be started by leaving Jane Austen out.

— Mark Twain

One must have a heart of stone to read the death of Little Nell without laughing.

— Oscar Wilde, on Charles Dickens's
The Old Curiosity Shop

Truman Capote has made lying an art. A minor art.

— Gore Vidal

Perhaps I have hit on a reason for my waning love of novels of which I was not aware before—that they have substituted gynecology for romance.

— Ben Hecht

Books like this drive one to class warfare, simply as a way of answering back.

— Michael Neve,
on Bernard Levin's *Enthusiasms*

Ms. [Germaine] Greer's most succinct descriptive writing is in the title of her book, which characterizes the text with precision.

— Brigid Brophy, on *The Obstacle Race:
The Fortunes of Women Painters and Their Work*

After years of gestation, this is his first novel, and the publisher's blurb describes it as having been "eagerly awaited." By whom, for heaven's sake?

— Charles Osborne, on Harold Brodkey's
The Runaway Soul

Thank you for the manuscript; I shall lose no time in reading it.

— Benjamin Disraeli's stock reply to authors who sent him
unsolicited copies of their works, attributed

From the moment I picked up your book until I laid it down, I was convulsed with laughter. Some day I intend reading it.

> — Groucho Marx, in a blurb for S. J. Perlman's
> *Dawn Ginsbergh's Revenge*

The covers of this book are too far apart.

> — Ambrose Bierce, attributed

Biography lends to death a new terror.

> — Oscar Wilde

Perhaps the greatest living American crime writer.

> — Stephen King, of George Pelecanos

"The style is what I have been talking about these several recent days: honest, simple, straight-forward, unostentatious, unbruffled [sic, a new coinage by Twain]; barren of impertinences & familiarities; dignified, refined, self-respectful & respectful toward the reader; bright, snappy, humorous, moving; & the story flows from the sources to the mouth without a break—& stays between the banks all the way, too. The characters are alive, & distinctly discriminated . . ."

> — Mark Twain, on the elements of good writing, commenting to
> Robert Barr on the author's novel *A Woman Intervenes*

The greatest novelist writing in English at the time of his death.

— Ian McEwan, of John Updike

H. L. Mencken. A comedian playing Hamlet.

— Irving Howe

As repressed sadists are supposed to become policemen or butchers, so those with irrational fear of life become publishers.

— Cyril Connolly

When you read a biography remember that the truth is never fit for publication.

— George Bernard Shaw

Don't be afraid of criticism. Anyone who can fill out a laundry slip thinks of himself as a writer. Those who can't fill out a laundry slip think of themselves as critics.

— George Seaton

All critics should be assassinated.

— Man Ray

The most stupendous event of my life.

— H. L. Mencken, about reading *The Adventures of Huckleberry Finn* at age nine

Any reviewer who expresses rage and loathing for a novel or a play or a poem is preposterous. He or she is like a person who has put on full armor and attacked a hot fudge sundae or a banana split.

— Kurt Vonnegut

My mother said that I must always be intolerant of ignorance but understanding of illiteracy. That some people, unable to go to school, were more educated and more intelligent than college professors.

— Maya Angelou

Almost every woman writer I know acknowledges a debt [to Doris Lessing.]

— Lisa Alther, attributed

It will bid fair to be the worst book ever written: smarmy, whiny, smirky and above all, almost indescribably stupid.

— Jonathan Yardley, on *At Home in the World*, by Joyce Maynard

He has never been known to use a word that might send a reader to the dictionary.

— William Faulkner, of Ernest Hemingway

Resources and References

Research also included mining various trade journals, newspapers and online sources, as well as personal interviews.

Atwan, Robert, and Donald McQuade. *The Writer's Presence*. Boston: Bedford Books, St. Martin's Press.

Bagdikian, Ben. *The Media Monopoly*. Boston: Beacon Press, 1983.

Bellow, Saul. *It All Adds Up*. New York: Viking, 1994.

Berg, A. Scott. *Max Perkins Editor of Genius*. New York: E. P. Dutton, 1978.

Burgess, Anthony. *99 Novels*. New York: Summit Books, 1984.

Cooke, Alistair. *The Vintage Mencken*. New York: Knopf (Vintage), 1955.

Dexter, Gary. *Poisoned Pens*. London: Frances Lincoln Limited, 2009.

Dillard, Annie. *The Writing Life*. New York: Harper & Row, 1989.

Donaldson, Sam. *Hold On, Mr. President*. New York: Random House, 1987.

Elledge, Scott. *E. B. White: A Biography*. New York: Norton, 1985.

Ellison, Ralph. *Going to the Territory*. New York: Random House, 1986.

Gill, Brendan. *Here at* The New Yorker. New York: Random House, 1975.

Glossbrenner, Alfred and Emily. *About the Author*. New York: Harcourt, 2000.

Gordimer, Nadine. *The Essential Gesture*. New York: Knopf, 1988.

Groth, Janet. *The Receptionist*. Chapel Hill: Algonquin Books of Chapel Hill, 2012.

Hall, Donald. *The Oxford Book of American Literary Anecdotes.* New York; Oxford University Press, 1981.

Hamill, Pete. *News is a Verb.* New York: Ballantine, 1998.

Higgins, George V. *On Writing.* New York: Henry Holt & Co, 1990.

James, P. D. *Time to Be in Earnest.* New York: Knopf, 2000.

Kempton, Murray. *Rebellions, Perversities, and Main Events.* New York: Times Books, 1994.

Kennedy, William. *Riding the Yellow Trolley Car.* New York: Viking, 1993.

Leonard, Elmore. *Elmore Leonard's 10 Rules of Writing.* New York: Harper Collins, 2007.

Lessing, Doris. *Under My Skin.* London: Harper Collins, 1994.

Levinson, Leonard Louis. *Bartlett's Unfamiliar Quotations.* Chicago: Henry Regnery Co., 1971.

MacDonald, Ross. *On Crime Writing.* Santa Barbara: Capra Press, 1973.

Mailer, Norman. *Advertisements for Myself.* New York: G. P. Putnam's Sons, 1959.

Maran, Meredith. *Why We Write.* New York: Plume, 2013.

McAlexander, Hubert H. *Conversations with Peter Taylor.* Jackson: University Press of Mississippi, 1987.

Morrell, Jessica Page. *Thanks, But This Isn't For Us.* New York: Penguin, 2009.

Parker, Robert B. *Parker on Writing.* Northridge: Lord John Press, 1985.

Patner, Andrew. *I. F. Stone: A Portrait.* New York: Pantheon Books, 1988.

Paul, Pamela. *By the Book.* New York: Henry Holt and Co., 2014.

Peters, Amy. *The Writer's Devotional.* New York: Sterling, 2012.

Phillips, Larry W. *Ernest Hemingway on Writing*. New York: Touchstone, 1999.

Rakoff, Joanna. *My Salinger Year*. New York: Knopf, 2014.

Schieffer, Bob. *This Just In: What I Couldn't Tell You on TV*. New York: G. P. Putnam's Sons, 2003.

Sipper, Ralph B. *Inward Journey*. Santa Barbara: Cordelia Editions, 1984.

Sloman, Larry. *On the Road with Bob Dylan*. New York: Three Rivers Press, 2002.

Smith, Larry. *The Moment*. New York: Harper Collins, 2012.

Stanton, Robert J., and Gore Vidal. *Views from a Window: Conversations With Gore Vidal*. Secaucus, NJ: Lyle Stuart, Inc., 1980.

Styron, William. *This Quiet Dust*. New York: Random House, 1982.

Talese, Gay. *A Writer's Life*. New York: Knopf, 2006.

Usher, Shaun. *Letters of Note*. San Francisco: Chronicle Books, 2013.

Ward, Laura. *Bad Press*. London: Baron's Educational Series, 2002.

Watkins, Floyd C., and John T. Hiers. *Robert Penn Warren Talking*. New York: Random House, 1980.

Welty, Eudora. *One Writer's Beginnings*. Cambridge: Harvard University Press, 1984.

White, Martha and E. B. White. *Letters of E. B. White, Revised Edition*. New York: Harper Collins, 2006.

Zinsser, William. *On Writing Well*. New York: Harper & Row, 1985.

Author Index

Peter Bollen, born in Lynn, Massachusetts, and raised there, has lived in Bridgton, Maine, since 2003.

He served in the U.S. Navy from 1968 to '70 and attended North Shore Community College in Beverly, MA. He was editor of the *Lynnfield Beacon*, a trade labor journal, and editor of the award-winning Labor journal, *Northeast News Service*, from 1989 to '96. Bollen's many essays and letters have appeared in newspapers and journals, including the *Salem Evening News*, the *Boston Herald*, the *Federal Times*, *North Shore Sunday*, the *Daily Item*, *Lake Living* magazine, and the *Bridgton News*.

Bollen initiated a lawsuit—eventually joined by more than a dozen plaintiffs—against the Justice Department to overturn a prohibition on compensation for freelance writing and speaking for all federal employees; the U.S. Supreme Court agreed and overturned the ban in 1995. He contributed a biography of the singer-songwriter Woody Guthrie to the Postmaster General in 1980, which helped result in a commemorative postage stamp of Guthrie as part of the Folk Musicians series.

Also by Peter Bollen: "Dear Bureaucrat"; *I Hold These Truths to Be Self Evident*, collected essays; and the short story, "Assignment: The Torch."

With Harry Sneakers Bollen